Just Breathe

For Steve and Joe

"An astonishing tour de force, guaranteed to ensure that you never again take for granted the automatic act of breathing, but fully appreciate how precious the 'sorcery' that 'conjures/life from thin air.' The act of breathing is also given a wider context, in which we are introduced to mechanics, science, the jargon of language, clean air, Covid failures and the animal kingdom.

But the overall joy of this collection is in its affirmation of humanity – a life in which Trish's sons refuse to be silenced, find joy in what they are able to do, play tricks on others, and despite a life that '… depends/on the flick of a switch', shows them 'burning brighter with each passing minute.'

You will be surprised, angered, educated, moved and ultimately inspired by the truth and life shining through this collection."

Cathy Grindrod

"*Just Breathe* bears unblinking witness to the most fundamental everyday fact of being able to breathe enough air to stay alive. Trish Kerrison energises the experience of a mother's struggle over two decades to keep her kids alive, set against the incessant ticking away of their breaths. A harrowing, provocative and necessary set of poems."

Ray Hearne

"Faint-heartedness has no place in Trish Kerrison's work – or indeed her life. An autobiographic odyssey pours strength on pages inked with authenticity and love."

Dr John Tams

"A collection about the first and last thing we do on this earth, woven beautifully through words which soar from the page, like a bird taking flight."

Sophie Sparham

Just Breathe
A story of life and breath

Trish Kerrison

> *tick tock*
> *tick tock*
> *count down a lifetime*
> *on a dandelion clock*

Five Leaves Publications
www.fiveleaves.co.uk
www.fiveleavesbookshop.co.uk

Just Breathe

Trish Kerrison

trishkerrison.org

Published in 2024 by Five Leaves Publications
14a Long Row, Nottingham NG1 2DH
www.fiveleaves.co.uk
www.fiveleavesbookshop. co.uk

ISBN: 978-1-915434-24-1

Copyright © Trish Kerrison 2024

Cover image copyright © Rebecca Evans
(R.A.E. Illustration) 2024

Printed in Great Britain

Contents

The Beaufort Scale of Breathing	7
First Breath	9
Between Breaths	11
Breathe Easy	12
Breath of Fresh Air	15
Deep Breath	16
Just Breathe	17
Breathing Space (1)	19
Holding My Breath	20
Sounds of Breathing	24
No Time to Draw Breath	25
Breathing Space (2)	26
Short of Breath	27
Breathing Space (3)	29
Puffed Out	30
Breathing Down His Neck	31
Almost Out of Breath	32
Completely Out of Breath	33
Masked	34
Breathing Space (4)	35
Fake Breaths	36
The Clean Air Act	37
Controlled Breathing	38
Breath-taking	39
The Spare	40
Scream	42
Breathing Space (5)	44
Bad Breath	45
Masquerade	46
Advice From the Department of Lung Function	48
Breathing Space (6)	50

Air Waves	51
Last Gasp	52
Memory Game (Part 1): Missing Piece	53
Memory Game (Part 2): Mental Arithmetic	54
Life Support	55
Breath of Life	56
Life and Breath	57
As I Live and Breathe	58
Acknowledgements	59

The Beaufort Scale of Breathing   [BSB rating]

10. STORM: Full ear-splitting force from the lungs of a hungry baby.
9. SEVERE GALE: Toddler fury when things don't go as planned.
8. GALE: Charge down the wing, yell to your mate for the pass.
7. NEAR GALE: Blow up a balloon, blow out every candle.
6. STRONG BREEZE: Play *Blow Wind Blow* on a tin whistle.
5. FRESH BREEZE: No coughing, sing *Happy Birthday to You*.
4. MODERATE BREEZE: Breaths shallow, no shouting.
3. GENTLE BREEZE: Speak softly, CO2 levels rising.
2. LIGHT BREEZE: Voice fading to a whisper.
1. LIGHT AIR: Not enough breath to live on.
0.

Breathe deep...

First Breath

I

The room holds its breath
countless seconds tick
tick
tick

already he is on his own

cast adrift with one sharp cut
lungs must get to work
or he will surely drown

ancestral memory stirs
Big Bang to fish,
fish to mammal

wet to dry

no going back.

A gasp
outrage at the cold
embrace of a waiting world.

His first breath
steals my breath away

II

And what of this air,
this nothing,
more precious than gold?

One cupful
enough for new-born lungs

one cup of gassy cocktail;
nitrogen, oxygen,
carbon dioxide, hydrogen,
a waft of neon –

how are new-born lungs to know
what to keep,
what to lose
at this, their very first diffusion?

Science gives no answers,
we must trust to ancient wisdoms,
to nature, to God,

to luck.

Muscles pull tight,
draw in the gaseous concoction,

a hundred million alveoli poised
to plunder its riches.
What sorcery is this that conjures
life from thin air?

III

Tiny toes, fingers, lips
turn pink, warm,
eyes open wide,
brighten.

We settle then,
content.
I breathe in
this moment
of his new life.

He sleeps
on my chest,
the rhythm
of my breaths

his familiar
lullaby.

Between Breaths

I know life's fragility,
spend long minutes
watching the rise
and fall of his tiny chest.
Listen,
night after night
to soft sounds shushing
through a monitor,

his breaths
my lullaby.

Breathe Easy

I

Wrapped up warm,
we sing 'Puff, the Magic Dragon'
all the way to playschool,
great clouds of breath
huffed into frosty air.

Inside, one deep breath, and…
the wheels on the bus
go round and round,
the mouse runs up the clock,
this little piggy goes to market,
atishoo, atishoo, we all fall down.

The wolf has breath enough,
huffs and puffs,
blows down houses
of straw or sticks,
but never the house of bricks.

Puff isn't everything.

Cheeks red,
short of breath,
we pant up the hill
and home.

II

Balloons of hot air
scrape the rooftop
roar with delight
as they rise towards   breath to spare
the clouds and away....   we blow bubbles   fragile rainbows
                                 in the garden   a moment's joy
                                                      floating

                         gone.

Hiccupping breaths
of disappointment
            (at this, or other heinous mother-crimes)
soothed by bathtime bubbles
clapped and splashed.

III

Why did the chicken cross the road?

...to get to the other side
...because she saw the zebra crossing
...to find her hat

a gaggle of small children
spill their giggles,
laugh at the discovery
of a joke of their own making
gasp for breath
each chicken funnier than the last,

no-one remembers where the joke started
no-one knows where it ends

...to catch a bus
...to have a picnic with the duck

joke after joke until bedtime
laughter filling a lifetime.

9 BSB

IV

Just enough breath,
birthday balloons
one for every party child
time running out.

Breathless
with excitement,
party games:
musical chairs,
pin the tail on the donkey,
pass the parcel,
let off steam,
run rings round the garden,

stop for breath

and cake.
Happy Birthday to you

five candles to blow out
gone
in one puff

Breath of Fresh Air

I

Six years old,
you yell till you're blue in the face
that big boys should stay up later,

then sink into pillows,
yawn as wide as a hippo's smile,
eyes shut tight
long before the wolf
gets his come-uppance.

II

Blood-curdling screams
in the dark
of the ghost train –
another birthday treat
with your mates.

Who was braver?
Who was scared-er?
Slurp down milkshake after
BURP, BURP…
Bigger, louder, go on!
I dare ya.

III

Hold your breath,
who does it longer
you or your brother?

Ten seconds, twenty, thirty?
bubbles burst
in shrieks of laughter.

Deep Breath

I

Chase around the playground
can't catch me
tig, tag, you're it
faster, faster,
only the lesson bell
will save ya.

Panting,
chest heaving
like Great-uncle Chain Smoker,
every breath a heavy labour;
like Grandad, TB on youthful lungs
stealing breath fifty years later.

Rest a moment
then off again
running down the field
for the joy of running.

run rabbit run

II

till you fall
      find your feet
             and fall
                    and fall again.

Just Breathe

I

Diagnosis: muscle failure
delivered by a medic in a single breath,
like ripping off a plaster,
it's better if done quicker:

wheelchair-ventilator-dead by eighteen

II

I no longer know how to
       breathe

                            a stutter

            a gulp

                a gasp   (is that me?)

Take a deep breath

       only

                         snatched

            shallow

                  breaths

                                come

as if I am
       stabbed

one deep
            breath
all it would take
       to twist   the knife   further   deeper
all the way
            in

III

breathe in
breathe   out
breathe in
breathe in
breathe   out
breathe in
is there any such rhythm
that can keep to the runaway scattergun beat
of a breaking heart?

Too dangerous to think,
fix the mind in the shallows
of the here and now
a small boy laughs as he plays,
still runs to his mum

tell the heart
it is enough

all I can do
is sit tight
tight-lipped
and hope to stumble

on a breathing space

Breathing Space (1)

with	even
one trachea	two bags of air
a pair of bronchi	miles of capillaries
half a billion alveoli	a multiplex of nerves
intercostal muscle lift	intrinsic respiratory drive
muscular effector system	diaphragm muscle stretch
a man must breathe the air	can't hold a breath too long
must breathe in and out or faint	the brain outwitting will-power
forcing fresh air into starving lungs	until breathing comes easy again

his muscle	if it fails
can't contract	to make a cavity
to expand a rib cage	to puff out his chest
to pull the diaphragm	no oxygen is drawn in
the lung is an empty bag	danger: risk of suffocation

Holding My Breath

    I

    A dozen candles

    blown and gone,

    one

    by

    one.

      Bleached lines

      on an x-ray

    reveal a spine

  that leans

    each month

      by degrees,

        twisting, curving

          to crush a heart,

            squash a lung.

        Function

        thirty percent

        and falling,

        air stagnating.

Ventilator on the shelf,
    winking,
clocks the wonky spine –
like a fox, eyes glinting,
clocking the open henhouse door –
bides its time.

II

The smallest window
left ajar to fix his spine
with nut, bolt, titanium rod,
surgical precision.
Lots of luck.

Last supper, first sitting
in the Rose and Crown,
scampi and chips
just how he likes it.

Breathless chatter,
still pretending to fool
ourselves that bad things
can't happen to us.

Dawn breaks,
he takes his chance.
Trusts a grown-up
to fix Meccano
vertebra to vertebra
in a twelve-hour game

of waiting.

III

We, and all who know him
hold our breaths
while hours tick slowly by,
day bleeds into twilight,
settles into night.

At last he sleeps
amidst drips, drains, machines,

he does not breathe.
The gentle shush and hush
of a ventilator does
the heavy lifting

for a day.
The habit of a lifetime
must not be broken,
a man must breathe alone.

In the drama of transition,
a line must be crossed, death to life,
machine back to human.

No-one dare take a single breath

until he gasps for air,
looks me in the eye.

*So Mum, he says,
I didn't die.*

And breathe...

Sounds of Breathing

A stethoscope, intuition,
a knowing pair of hands
to understand
the percussion of a troubled lung.

The dull thud of   dead space
where air no longer passes.

The whistle and wheeze
of air squeezing
through a tiny gap.

How to tap and shake
with drummer's skill –
stick to the beat, single stroke,
roll or double, front to back,
back to front, side-to-side,
vibrate, listen,
wait

for a rip-roaring crackle,
loud and coarse
obstruction shifting,
something softer, finer
until,
a whoosh of air

finds its way,
settles
to a gentle rustle

breathed in
breathed out.

No Time to Draw Breath

I

No stopping for a breather,
brother and sister roped together
pull a buggy up a hillside
all the way to the top of the world
for no more reward
than a chocolate bar
and a breathtaking view that lasts forever.

II

Enough breath
to add a voice
to a Wembley roar:
Come on you Rams!
and sing a victory song
all the miles home.

III

Like a football team
one goal adrift, lungs do not
throw in the towel, but rather
fight on to the death – find
other ways to breathe, gulp
and swallow, or stack each breath
one on top of the other

before letting go.

Breathing Space (2)
Other Ways to Breathe

think of a fish
a dart through water
absorbing oxygen
in a graceful flow
of efficiency

think of a frog
basking in sunshine
inhaling air
through lungs much like yours or mine
until a threat
he dives
and like a superhero we don't believe in
switches dry mode to wet
outsmarts the villain
breathes through his skin

think too of a sparrow
dismissed as dull
her lungs are a wonder
always full
air sacs like bellows
maintain a crazy metabolic rate
four hundred heartbeats a minute
or more
as she soars through the heavens
singing

Short of Breath

I

Why does a man need his cough?
Something frivolous perhaps
the announcement of his own importance
to the boardroom, a waiter, his audience,
or is it for vital airway-clearance?

Alert to danger,
muscle responds to reflex
as best it can – feeble efforts
over and over and over.

II

There are those *cough* who should *cough* know better,
who failed *cough* to consider the *cough* evidence,
who do not *cough* live with the *cough* consequences,
who cling *cough* to their belief *cough* that a cough
is a luxury *cough* that the N *cough* HS can ill *cough* afford,
so eighty *cough* thousand pounds is *cough* spent
in five *cough* days on intensive care *cough* compared
with five cough thousand pounds *cough*
for a cough-assist machine *cough* that would *cough*
solve the coughing problem *cough* and keep him
out *cough* of hospital *cough* for years.

III

Sitting in intensive care,
my breaths adjust to the steady
puff of his ventilator. In my hand,
the letter:

re cough assistor

*no clinical trial has been undertaken to prove
its use in lung-muscle failure, therefore,
he does not meet funding criteria. If his
condition was rarer, his needs more
than another's, there would be grounds
to reconsider.*

We understand that you may be disappointed.

IV

**Proposal for a clinical trial to evaluate
the efficacy of a cough-assistance machine
in advanced Duchenne Muscular Dystrophy:**

> Enlist two affected teenagers.
> Randomly select one for cough-assistance.
> Note who dies first.

V

A dragon with fire on its breath
cannot match the fury of a mother
whose son looked death right in the eye
because the NHS pie isn't big enough
and tough decisions must be made.

Did you do yourself a favour,
did you vote for lower taxes?
And are you absolutely sure
that when the line in the sand is drawn,
it won't be you that gets cut off?

Breathing Space (3)
Everybody, Take a Breath

Humans should take lessons
in how not to forget
the things that matter,

like the Great Smog of 1952
that choked a capital
into a Clean Air Act,
a serious inconvenience to business
but a great relief to the lungs of the city,

or the Smoking Act of 2007
that gave space to fresh air
and blew smoke in the face
of poison for profit,

paved the way to wearing
a good jacket to the pub,

moved the fug two hundred yards
further away from the hospital door.

But humans, being humans,
shout about the Nanny State
and assaults on freedom,
as if we all had a craving
to wheeze our way to death.

Puffed Out

His lungs have had their fill of airs
blown in from far and near:
balmy Southerlies, brutal North Easterlies,
warm breezes from Mediterranean seas,
breaths clean with knife-edge sharpness
from the snow peak of the Zugspitze,
gaseous gulps, dense and sulphurous,
from the smoke plumes of Vesuvius,
but his lungs are now all out of puff,
need the bluff and bluster of his mates
to blow out the eighteen candles
on his birthday cake, while we,
watching from the wings,
know which way the wind is blowing.

Breathing Down His Neck

I am she:
stuff of your nightmares, villain, ventilator,
demon, breathing machine, life-saver…

It's high time you looked me in the eye.

You pretend you have no need of me,
leave me, boxed-up, in a cupboard,
denounce me as the enemy,

while I, with infinite patience,
forgive your naivety, your belief
that nature's faults can be held
in abeyance, your hope that time
can be slowed, or even stopped

but the game is up.

From the shadows, I observe
the change; his breaths rapid, shallow.
It's time to make my move,
to become his closest friend,
one he can depend on
for life.

Almost Out of Breath

Lungs bear their scars
like the broken-hearted:
a quiet struggle in the night,
refusal to accept the inevitable,

it's so hard to ask for help

to surrender to this enemy
pretending to be friend.

Fifteen years

for lungs to give up the fight
to signal an intention
to negotiate
a dignified settlement:

night-time assistance only.

Out of sight, out of mind
dawn till dusk.

No fuss.

4 BSB

Completely Out of Breath

Gracious in nocturnal victory,
she lets us believe the ship
is steady, that she brings
calm waters. Like a gentle tide,

she laps at the foot of the cliff,
silently claims new territory
inch by inevitable inch,
minute by inevitable minute.

Before we know it,
eight hours slips
to eight-and-a-half, nine,

then the storm hits
and there she is,
offering her services
as the cliff collapses.

No strength left for resistance,
nine hours become sixteen,

night drifts into day.
No longer confined to her room
she tags along with us

everywhere

like some annoying old aunt
determined to be 'of use'.

3 BSB

Masked

The face behind the mask is me.
You may see the odd photo
without it (for Mum)
but it leaves its mark.
We'll not be parted long.

It's no big deal, except the tube,
bright white, clinical, stark
against the black of my 'Rebellion
Festival' shirt as if the designer
couldn't imagine a life outside
a hospital.

It scares people, which is weird,
it's only air. They stare for ages
or look away, then jump sky high
when I shout HELLO
through my microphone,
just so they know that I am here.

My mask, my interface
between breath and death.
No more. No less.

Breathing Space (4)
The Question of Breathing

Is the patient breathing? The first question they ask. The only question that really matters. It is hard not to breathe, we are wired for life. For most, ninety seconds is all the brain allows before it sends its Mayday message to breathless lungs: *Breathe! Breathe!* And so the feeble effort of willpower is swiftly brushed aside. But in our imperfect world, not every SOS is heard. Not a failure of intent, just a failure of mechanics. Not part of a global or Godly plot, nor a cause for pity, not a means by which human frailty may be measured and judged, nothing but a genetic accident and a strict adherence to the laws of physics.

Fake Breaths

I

Mercury, chromium, cadmium,
beryllium, lithium, lead,
the world is scoured and mined
for the making of a thousand parts:
motherboards, lights, switches,
bellows, batteries, alarms,
four kilograms of dead weight
round his neck in exchange
for a breath of air,

weightless,

loaded with oxygen,
ready for the taking.

II

Where does it go
this treasure,
this oxygen?

How puny now seem
opium routes, saffron trails, silk roads,
their journeys fools' errands
for worthless trinkets

beside this life-giving cargo
pumped one full circuit,
heart back to heart,
in less than sixty seconds' run.

The Clean Air Act

He takes the air
double-filtered

in rationed parcels
delivered with a piquancy

of plastic, a soupçon
of silicone

every breath tainted
by the whiff of mechanics.

Oxygen is oxygen
his lungs make no complaint.

Controlled Breathing

The unchanging rhythm
of a rosary, a mantra,
an incantation –
        five seconds in
        five seconds out
– for the good of the body
and the soul

the steady breaths of conversation,
breathless declarations, pauses
for dramatic effect, for punchlines

Why did the chicken cross the road?

…I don't know, ask the chicken

a long slow exhalation
across fourteen beats of a note
pushed out from the diaphragm,
sustained to fill a room,
a theatre, a stadium

the full force of a pair of lungs
emptied into clarinet, bagpipe,
recorder, French horn, each breath
stretched out to carry the world
on a wave of sound

or breath control by machine, the

length of in and out dictated so that

each sentence is broken into pieces

of the exact same duration so people

assume that he has finished speaking

and so jump right in with their thoughts, theories, ideas, jokes, judgements, words
of wisdom, homilies, hot gossip, speculation, conclusions, unstoppable opinions

when in fact there is so much more

that he needs to say.

Breath-taking

Without so much as a by-your-leave,
her victory is complete:
assisted breathing
to life-dependency
in three short years.

She has outdone herself,
cannot now be relied upon
to deliver on her promises –
always, everywhere,
must bring a friend, a spare
just in case.

The Spare

A few moments, please
I'm initializing...

Please wait...

While you are waiting
please attend to the following:
check I'm fully charged,
pack my spare batteries
fetch my designer bag
the waterproof one with extra padding,
inspect the breathe tube for leaks
you know how it splits in the heat
and make sure you've got the right mask,
we don't want a repeat of last week.

I'll you let know when I'm ready
watch for the flash of green lights
on my client-friendly interface.

Please wait...

What do you mean
you can't be bothered to wait,
you'll just use Vent One
as she's already turned on?

We had an agreement!

I'm Vent Two, daytime settings,
Vent One is nights only,
extra pressure, remember?

Oh, so she has the tech to switch
her settings, how very clever.

So, you plan to abandon me
in the back of the car, on stand-by,
just in case she decides she's had enough
and packs up early?

It's offensive, that's what it is.

I guess I'll just have to wait,
until you really need me at my best,
a wedding perhaps, or a funeral,
or that hold-your-breath moment
in the front row of the cinema,

then I'll flash all my red lights
and alarm, and alarm, and alarm
for no reason.

I've cheered myself up just thinking about it.

Still want to leave me in the car?

Scream

one a.m.
a scream
loud enough to wake the dead
on and on and on

adrenaline flood
heart pump
run rabbit run

four-minute warning?
alien invasion?
divine retribution?

or a ventilator
stuck in a start-up loop

initialise…
fail
scream the house down for two minutes

try again
try again
try again

until the internal battery dies
at six a.m.

software failure, apparently,
a glitch, happens every now and then,
no cause for alarm

And breathe again...

Breathing Space (5)
Don't Hold Your Breath

governments deny everything
commercial behemoths bandy words
of carefully planned power cuts
in neat chessboard patterns,
of emergency blackouts,
of a register alerting authorities
of threats to quarterly profits

trust no-one
to whom you are
an account number

when push comes to shove
and the power goes off
they are 'them'
we are 'us'

explaining
'life' and 'death'
to a chatbot

Bad Breath

A world turns on its head:
a comic-book dragon roars
in the Chinese quarter,
venom on her breath,
and we clear her way
as if we modern humans
need have no fear
of plague.

Weak-chested; he's on their list
for a letter, seven pages:
stay at home, stay at home, stay at home,
signed 'Matt'.

We draw our own conclusions
policy and practice lay bare
the truth:

the bed in intensive care
is reserved for more deserving cases

he spits in their face
dyes his hair purple
parties back to life
at summer festivals

outdoors

not too close.

Masquerade

I

Anyone could be anyone behind a mask:
superhero or villain, genius or fool,
hot under the collar, cool as a cucumber,
laughing with you,
or at you.

II

It's been trendy, of late, to wear
a mask, an act of neighbourliness

strangely condemned in some quarters
as a co-ordinated attempt

to deny the masses freedom
to catch a deadly virus

despite the fact that those in charge
proved, month after month,

the only thing they could organise
was a piss-up.

III

How carelessly the man in charge
let the mask slip – from contrite
to self-righteous, from man of the people
to every man for himself, from levelling up
to cleaning up, here to help,
to help yourself.

Of all the masks he could have worn
he chose to wear none at all
in public places, exposed
his true face.

IV

Unmasked, our leaders
continue their masquerade
of governance

wash their hands
of responsibility

hide scientific fact
behind dumb rhetoric
of heroic battles won

we have our trusty shields,
we will not succumb

two hundred and twenty thousand lives
lost
and still counting

costly inquiries
waste their breath

those who politicked

partied

profited

through a plague
of failings

now reap their reward – vast sums
paid for after-dinner speeches.

Everyone applauds.

Advice from the Department of Lung Function

The shape of breath

is changing.

Circle to triangle?
Square to oval?

Let me explain…

This old lady, she bellows out
basic old-fashioned breaths
from a sturdy white box,
reliable any way up, stoic,
like your Grandma,
but such a sluggard

She takes an age to reach maximum pressure
Like a long slow drag up to a mountain top
before dropping off
then sliding the scree

But this ultra-modern Miss
(courtesy of post-COVID interest
in profits to be made from
other ways of breathing)

keeps her breaths contained
in a precious white case,
light-weight, pretty, with an air
of fragility – a diva, with demands,
stand her upright – or she quits
but she's efficient, none-the-less

she builds quickly up to the peak, maintaining full pressure *before exhalation*
climbing so steeply *then striding onward along the ridge* *to a rapid descent*

    so much to be gained
    from an upgrade:
    optimised breathing
    for living your best life
    varied pressures for day
    and night, humidifier built-in,
    infinite adjustments, remote
    monitoring, slot in battery

    but perhaps I jump the gun,
    after all these years
    can you now go
    with a modern ebb and flow?

    YEAH, WHATEVER.

Breathing Space (6)
Breathing New Life into Old Language

Peak: the summit of mountains climbed,
Blencathra, Scafell, Red Pike.
Flow: the exuberance of ice-melt
streams rushing over weary feet.
Air Pressure: lines on a weather map,
Grandad tapping his barometer.
Tidal: all things swept up in the dance
of moon and earth and sea.

Poetics must give way to function,
words pared back for mechanics.
Peak flow a measure of exhalation,
tidal volume sizes up the breath
taken in, *air pressure* now a matter
of choice. Touch screen to reset.

The technician explains the benefits
of the new and improved, as far as
jargon will allow. But his words fail him,
fail us. He steals then, from the poet,
talks of '*the changing shape of breath*'
as if we always knew that breath
was a shape-shifting thing.

Air Waves

Only here does the sound
make sense

that incessant noise in
his head

the break of a wave on
a beach

no high tide or neap tide
no storm

to alter its volume
or shape

to make it rage or scream
or dance

or make it recede to
nothing

unless he holds onto
a breath

just for the fun of it

to trigger an alarm
and watch them run

Last Gasp

NINE-NINE-NINE

    oxygen falling
      pulse dropping
        heart failing
          out of time
                just breathe…just breathe…just breathe…
      ventilator flashes red,
      screams a cacophony

AIRWAY BLOCKED

AIRFLOW STOPPED

OUT OF BREATH

    life on a knife-edge

    common cold
        to
    common death

                unless…

    a desperate shake of the chest

    something gives

    he lives.

            And…   breathe.

1 BSB

Memory Game (Part 1): Missing Piece

Can you remember this?

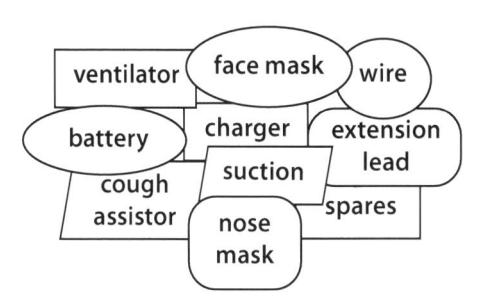

[diagram showing overlapping shapes labeled: ventilator, face mask, wire, battery, charger, extension lead, cough assistor, suction, nose mask, spares]

Something missing?

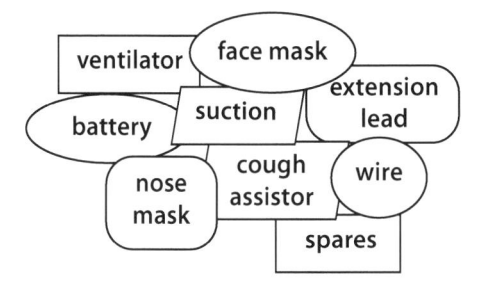

[diagram showing overlapping shapes labeled: ventilator, face mask, extension lead, battery, suction, nose mask, cough assistor, wire, spares]

Junction 17, M6.
One hour and twenty-six minutes from home.

Wanna risk it?

Memory Game (Part 2): Mental Arithmetic

Let's be scientific about this.
2 ventilators equals 12 hours' power $\quad\quad\quad\quad$ **2 x 6 = 12**
plus a battery for an extra 6 hours, which makes 18 $\quad\quad$ **+ 6 = 18**
clearly enough for a day out.
90 minutes' drive each way takes up 3 hours, $\quad\quad\quad$ **− 3 = 15**
but maybe we'll have to stop for fuel, a drink,
take 1 more hour off for that, $\quad\quad\quad\quad\quad\quad\quad\quad$ **− 1 = 14**
and what about being stuck in traffic?
(you really can't trust a Google Map)
Another hour perhaps, so now we're down to 13, $\quad\quad$ **− 1 = 13**
and if we stay from 10 til 6, that will take 8 more, $\quad\quad$ **− 8 = 5**
giving a comfortable 5 hours spare.
All good, but what if the ventilator fails?
That would wipe out 6 hours $\quad\quad\quad\quad\quad\quad\quad\quad$ **− 6 = ⎡−1⎤ !**
so now we're into minus breaths,
whatever they are.
OK, that'd be unlucky, even by our standards, but $\quad\quad$ **OR**
just suppose the car breaks down instead,
and rescue takes 2 hours to arrive, so we're left with 3, $\quad$ **5 − 2 = 3**
then, if they can't fix us on the spot,
we have to wait $\quad\quad\quad\quad\quad\quad\quad\quad\quad\quad\quad\quad$ **?????**
for a towing truck,
and they have no idea if they can even locate
a vehicle to take his wheelchair.

Well,
then we're fucked. $\quad\quad\quad\quad\quad\quad\quad\quad\quad\quad\quad$ ***!?**%!?***

Life Support

Every back-up plan must have its plan B,
C, D… along with so much paraphernalia
that I yearn for an old-fashioned railway porter
to weave a trolley through the crowds of people,
like in a black and white film, shouting
Mind your backs, please, while they,
well-versed in the game,
step out of his way.

But here, in the real world,
no slack is granted to the over-burdened,
rules have been abandoned,
the disabled parking bay
taken by someone who thinks
'disability' means not wanting to walk
too far in the rain, and polite requests
to grant safe passage to those
who need a wider road are met
with planted feet and a terse reminder that
we are all in the same boat.

A young man, a hero in any age,
steps forward,
asks, '*And what boat might that be, madam?*'

An eye on the camera in his hand,
she swears, steps away.

Breath of Life

Mic-ed up, surrounded by his gang of mates,
he sings with the band, every exhalation
spent giving life to the raucous anthems
that span his twenty-eight years.

A ventilator can't silence him.

The cake arrives crowned with sparking, spitting,
fizzing firework candles – an unquenchable spirit
captured on camera, refusing to be dimmed,
burning brighter with each passing minute.

Life and Breath

The gods of life breathed air   into the lungs of all creation.
                           So man has believed for all time.

              A man lives,   therefore he breathes.
              He breathes,   therefore he lives,

but if he breathes through a machine,
                           is his life any less divine?

           If his breath is parcelled
                       in a small white box,
     is it Frankenstein's creation
                   or the work of the gods?

Is he less alive
because he can no longer breathe alone,

                               or more alive
            because he tight-ropes on the edge of here
                                  and gone?

As I Live and Breathe

We, who breathe easy,
cannot know
what it is

to live
on the cusp of a breath,

to trust
to wire, battery, motherboard
to inflate waiting lungs

to rely
on someone
never getting it wrong,

to know
that life depends
on the flick of a switch.

Can we, who breathe easy
ever fully comprehend

what it means to live?

Acknowledgements

With thanks to:

Pippa Hennessy and all at Five Leaves for their belief in my second poetry project and for their sterling work in bringing it to fruition.

MY TEAM: Steve, Joe, Emma, Rob and Mark – for hard work, humour and the sheer bloody-mindedness which keeps the whole show on the road.

Cathy Grindrod, my poetry mentor, for wisdom and poetic knowledge generously shared.

Members of Nottingham Writer Highway and Ripley Writers, for helpful comments, inspiration and friendship.

Dr John Tams, songmaker, musician, storyteller – without whom my inner poet may never have surfaced, for his valuable insights into all things writing, and his unerring belief in my ability to tell my stories.

Rebecca Evans, for the stunning cover illustration.

Ray Hearne and Sophie Sparham for poetic comradeship.

The Respiratory and Lung Function Departments at Queen's Medical Centre, Nottingham, for every breath.

Also from Five Leaves: New Poetry

Five Leaves presents a new series of debut poetry pamphlets by East Midlands writers, showcasing the exciting range of emerging talent from our region.

1. *She Will Allow Her Wings* Jane Bluett
   978-1-915434-09-8, 40 pages, £7, June 2023
2. *Beyond Caring* Trish Kerrison
   978-1-915434-10-4, 40 pages, £7, September 2023
3. *North by Northnorth* Elvire Roberts
   978-1-915434-12-8, 44 pages, £7, December 2023
4. *The Stories In Between* Teresa Forrest
   978-1-915434-11-1, 32 pages, £7, December 2023
5. *Keep All the Parts* Roy Young
   978-1-915434-13-5, 34 pages, £7, March 2024
6. *Relief Map* Jan Norton
   978-1-915434-14-2, 33 pages, £7, March 2024
7. *New Uses for a Wand* Fiona Theokritoff
   978-1-915434-16-6, 40 pages, £7, June 2024
8. *You Worry Too Much* Nathan Fidler
   978-1-915434-17-3, 32 pages, £7, June 2024
9. *Kindling* Julie Burke
   978-1-915434-19-7, 44 pages, £7, September 2024
10. *Remembering* Julie Gardner
    978-1-915434-20-3, 40 pages, £7, September 2024
11. *Full Body Reclaim* Caroline Stancer
    978-1-915434-25-8, 40 pages, £7, December 2024

All of our books can be ordered from our websites.

Five Leaves Publications/Bookshop
14a Long Row, Nottingham NG1 2DH   0115 837 3097
info@fiveleaves.co.uk   bookshop@fiveleaves.co.uk
www.fiveleaves.co.uk   www.fiveleavesbookshop.co.uk